MW00774454

GLUTEN-FREE DAIRY-FREE EGG-FREE

Recipes

Oasis-Kitchen.com

Rita Mustafa, Holistic Nutritionist

ISBN : 978-0-9867558-1-1

Printed in Canada

The information presented in this book is based on the training, experience and research of the author. The suggestions in this book are not intended as a substitute for consulting with your health care provider.

Published by Art Book Bindery, Winnipeg, Manitoba

Photographs by MARLON P.| PHOTOGRAPHY
www.marlonpphoto.com

Wholesale Orders:

Quantity discounts are available for nutritionists, naturopathic doctors, bookstores and health food stores.

Copies can be ordered online at www.OasisHealth.ca or by calling 416-312-7617.

Contents

Recipes

When diet is wrong medicine is of no use.
When diet is correct medicine is of no need.
- Ancient Ayurvedic Proverb

Introduction

As long as I can remember, I have always been interested in health and nutrition. Although I thought I was living a healthy lifestyle by being vegetarian it still left me suffering from recurring sinus infections, digestive problems, fatigue and headaches. This eventually led me to seek answers that did not involve popping pills and medications. Today, as a Holistic Nutritionist I have combined my knowledge, passions and experiences to help other people achieve better health through nutrition.

This cookbook is a collection of gluten-free, dairy-free and egg-free recipes which I use in my home and have been tried, tested and , shared with many clients.

Although this book was created for those with food allergies, sensitivities and intolerances, it also dedicated to those who choose to eat a whole-food, plant-based diet as well.

More and more people are beginning to realize the benefit of following a plant-based diet.

Following a whole-food, plant-based diet simply means eating more whole-plant foods such as beans, vegetables, fruit, nuts and seeds, and avoiding animal foods.

Many chronic diseases are related to the choices we make every day. By adopting a healthier lifestyle that includes plant-based foods and physical activity, you can help keep disease at bay.

Whether you have food allergies or intolerances or just choose to eat more healthful foods, I hope you enjoy the recipes provided.

Substitutions

Switching to allergen-free cooking requires some adjustment, including the use of new ingredients—possibly some that you have never heard of before.

The substitutions used in this book are as follows.

Gluten

Gluten is a protein found in grains (wheat, rye, barley, spelt and kamut). This cookbook was tested using the following gluten-free mixture.

Gluten-Free Flour Mix

1 ½ cups brown rice flour

1 ½ cups sorghum flour

1 cup tapioca starch or arrowroot powder

Combine all ingredients and store in airtight container.

SUBSTITUTIONS: Brown rice flour and or sorghum flour can replaced, in whole or in part, with any other gluten-free flour such as quinoa, teff, buckwheat, millet, amaranth or bean flour.

NOTE: Pre-packaged gluten-free flour blends can be purchased at any health food store. If the flour blend you purchase contains xanthan gum or other gums, then additional xanthan gum or guar gum listed in these recipes will not be required.

Oats

Oats do not contain gluten but are frequently processed in the same facilities as gluten products. For those who suffer from celiac disease, look for oats that are certified gluten-free.

Substitutions

Milk / Dairy

Substituting cow's milk can easily be done by replacing it with one of the many dairy-free beverages on the market today, such as rice milk, almond milk, hemp milk or coconut milk.

You can also make your own dairy free milk which will keep well in the refrigerator for three or four days.

Almond Milk
1 cup almonds, soaked in water overnight and strained
4 cups water
6 dates
1 tsp. pure vanilla extract

In a blender add soaked almonds water, dates and vanilla.
Blend on high speed for 1 minute.
Strain the almond mixture using a cheesecloth.

Eggs

Eggs have many roles in baking such as leavening and binding.
The following egg substitute will provide some of the properties of an egg and are used in several recipes throughout this cookbook.

Flax Egg Replacement (*replacement for 1 egg*)
1 tbsp. ground flax seeds
3 tbsp. water

In a small pot, whisk together the flax seeds and water. Simmer 5 minutes over medium-low heat, stirring often, until mixture thickens to the consistency of egg whites. Cool completely before using.

NOTE: you can double or triple the recipe and freeze in ice cube trays for later use. Thaw before using.
(1 egg = 2 tablespoons of flax mixture)

Ingredients Used in this Cookbook

The ingredients used in this cookbook are readily available at your local health food stores and large chain supermarkets.

Agave Syrup (RAW)

Agave syrup, also called nectar, is a sweet, concentrated syrup made from the Agave plant. Read labels carefully and look for raw agave syrup, which means the agave was not heated during processing. Otherwise, it is highly processed and therefore not recommended.

Substitutions: honey, coconut nectar, maple syrup, brown rice syrup

Almond Butter

A nut butter made from ground almonds. Almond butter is available crunchy or smooth, and may be labeled either raw or roasted, describing the almonds themselves prior to grinding.

Substitutions: any other nut or seed butter

Almond Milk

Almond milk is a dairy-free milk made from almonds. Almond milk is now available in the dairy section of your grocery store as well as in shelf stable containers on grocery store and health food store shelves. It is also very easy to make your own almond milk for a fraction of the cost (*page 7*).

Substitutions: *rice milk, hemp milk, coconut milk*

Apple Cider Vinegar (RAW)

Apple cider vinegar is made by the fermentation of apple cider. Look for organic, raw and unfiltered for the best health benefits.

Bragg Liquid Soy Seasoning

A liquid protein concentrate, derived from soybeans, which is unfermented and gluten free. Visit www.bragg.com for information.

Substitutions: gluten-free soy sauce, coconut aminos

Ingredients Used in this Cookbook

Brown Rice Flour
Brown rice flour is milled from unpolished brown rice so it has a higher nutritional value and fibre content than white rice.

Buckwheat Flour
Buckwheat is not, despite its name, a form of wheat. Buckwheat is actually related to rhubarb. The small seeds of the plant are ground to make this flour.

Cocoa Beans or Cacao Beans
The raw cacao bean, the same bean used to make chocolate, is one of nature's most fantastic superfoods and is remarkably high in magnesium. Look for them in your local health food store.

Cocoa Butter or Cacao Butter
Cacao butter is the pure oil of the cacao bean. It is essential for making chocolate, and it has many other delicious uses, too, in baked goods and raw treats.

Visit www.navitasnaturals.com to order online or visit your favourite health food store.

Cocoa Powder
Natural unsweetened cocoa powder gives a deep chocolate flavor to baked goods. For those following a raw food diet, RAW cocoa powder can be substituted.

Coconut Flour
Coconut flour is made from pure, white, fresh coconut meat. It is high in dietary fibre, low in digestible carbohydrates, a good source of protein and free of gluten.

Ingredients Used in this Cookbook

Coconut Milk (canned)
Canned coconut milk is made from the pressing of fresh, ripe coconut meat.

Coconut Milk (beverage)
Coconut milk beverage is a wonderful dairy alternative but is not recommended in recipes that call for canned coconut milk.

Coconut Oil
Used as a healthy substitute for shortening and butter.
- Choose **extra virgin coconut oil** for recipes where coconut taste and smell is required. Otherwise, choose **expeller pressed** coconut oil, which is not refined using chemical solvents.
- Avoid coconut oil labeled as refined.

Coconut Sugar (*also known as Palm Sugar*)
This pure and simple sugar is made from the flower bud of the coconut tree.
Substitutions: sucanat sugar, date sugar

Dates
There are endless varieties of dates grown. You can easily find dried dates at your local grocery store or health food store and they are usually quite inexpensive. Medjool dates, are considerably more expensive, and are specifically called for in several of the recipes in this cookbook.

Gluten-free Bread Crumbs
Gluten-free bread crumbs are easily available at your favourite health food store. Instead of paying premium price for them, consider making your own by using stale gluten-free bread or gluten-free crackers. Just process them in your food processor or blender until you have fine crumbs.

Ingredients Used in this Cookbook

Gluten-free Flour Mix
Pre-packaged gluten-free flour blends can be purchased at any health food store. It is also very easy to make your own gluten-free flour mix for a fraction of the cost. (*page 6*)

Goji Berries
Goji berries have a mild tangy taste that is slightly sweet and sour. They have a similar shape and texture to raisins. Goji berries are rich in antioxidants and are considered a superfood.

Guar Gum
Guar gum is used in gluten-free baking for its thickening and binding properties. Guar gum is extracted from the guar bean and is available at any health food store.
Substitutions: xanthan gum

Hemp Seeds
A whole food, containing essential fatty acids (EFAs), protein, fibre, carbohydrates, natural vitamins and minerals but no cholesterol. The ratio of Omega 3 and Omega 6 EFAs in the oil component are in perfect balance for human health.

Medjool Dates
Medjool dates, often called the king of dates, are most sought after for their size and rich, intensely sweet flavour. Medjool dates are available in grocery stores and health food stores.

Nori
A type of edible seaweed that is dried or toasted, and sold in sheets. Available in most grocery stores.

Ingredients Used in this Cookbook

Quinoa
While quinoa is usually considered a whole grain, it is actually a seed. This nutrient-rich grain is a wonderful source of protein and dietary fiber.

Rice Milk
Rice milk is a dairy-free milk made from rice. Rice milk is now available in the dairy section of your grocery store as well as in shelf stable containers on grocery store and health food store shelves.
Substitutions: almond milk, hemp milk, coconut milk

Safflower Oil (High Oleic)
Different oils have different uses, and each performs best within a certain range of temperatures. High oleic safflower oil a great option when looking for a neutral flavored oil for baking.
Substitutions: coconut oil

Sea Salt
Harvested from evaporated seawater, sea salt receives little or no processing, leaving it rich in minerals. It is a healthier alternative to refined table salt.

Sorghum Flour
Sorghum is a whole grain flour and is high in fibre and protein. This flour works very well in baked goods such as muffins and breads and is a key ingredient in my gluten-free flour mix (*page 6*).
This flour is available at health food stores.

Spirulina Powder
Spirulina is a blue-green algae and is a rich source of protein, vitamins, minerals, carotenoids, and antioxidants. Look for this in the supplement aisle of your health food store.

Ingredients Used in this Cookbook

Tahini (Sesame Butter)

There are two main varieties of sesame butter: the Asian variety, which is called sesame butter and is usually raw, and the Middle Eastern variety, which is called tahini and is made with roasted seeds. Either will work in the recipes provided.

Tapioca Flour or Starch

Tapioca flour is made from the root of the cassava plant. Once ground, it takes the form of a light, soft, fine white flour. Tapioca flour adds chewiness to baking and is a good thickener.

Thai Red or Green Curry Paste

A prepared curry paste made with fresh chilis, lemongrass and thai ginger. For more information visit www.thaikitchen.com

Unsweetened Coconut

Unsweetened coconut can be found in a variety of forms from shredded to large flakes, at your local health food store.

Note: *sweetened coconut sold in grocery stores is made by taking the desiccated coconut and soaking it in corn syrup and preservatives. Therefore, it is not recommended.*

Xanthan Gum

Used in gluten-free cooking to bind, thicken and emulsify. Xanthan gum is a corn-based, fermented product and can be substituted with guar gum for those with sensitivities to corn. Both xanthan gum and guar gum can be found at any health food store.

BREAKFAST & SNACK FOODS

Buckwheat Pancakes

Despite its name, buckwheat (also known as kasha) is not related to wheat. Buckwheat is high in quality plant proteins, antioxidants, dietary fibre and minerals.

2 cups rice milk
2 tsp. apple cider vinegar
1 tsp. vanilla extract
1 tbsp. raw agave syrup
1 tbsp. safflower oil or melted coconut oil
1 ¾ cups buckwheat flour
1 tbsp. baking powder
Pinch of sea salt
Coconut oil for cooking

In a small bowl, combine milk, vinegar, vanilla, agave syrup and oil.

In a separate bowl, combine flour, baking powder and salt.

Slowly whisk the rice milk mixture into the flour mixture until you have a smooth batter. Allow batter to sit 10-15 minutes.

Preheat a skillet over medium heat.
Generously coat skillet with coconut oil before cooking each pancake.

Pour ¼ cup of batter into skillet and cook until bubbles begin to appear.

Flip pancake and continue to cook until golden brown on the bottom.

Transfer to a warming plate and repeat with remaining batter.

Serve topped with fresh fruit, nuts, maple syrup or agave syrup.

Serves 4-6

Pumpkin Spice Muffins

Pumpkin is not only nutritious but adds moisture and a natural sweetness to many gluten free recipes.

Muffin

1 cup rice milk
1 tsp. apple cider vinegar
1 ½ cups gluten free flour mix (*page 6*)
½ tsp. xanthan gum or guar gum
½ tsp. baking soda
1 ½ tsp. baking powder
⅛ tsp. sea salt
½ tsp. cinnamon
½ tsp. nutmeg
¼ tsp. allspice
¼ cup coconut sugar
½ cup safflower oil or melted coconut oil
½ cup canned or homemade pumpkin puree (*page 64*)
1 tsp. vanilla extract
1 tbsp. coconut flour

Spiced Topping

¼ cup walnuts, crushed
2 tbsp. coconut sugar
½ tsp. cinnamon

Prepare topping by combining walnuts, coconut sugar and cinnamon together.

Preheat oven to 375°F.
Line 12-cup muffin pan with paper liners.

In a measuring cup, combine rice milk and vinegar and set aside.

In a large bowl, add gluten free flour, xanthan gum, baking soda, baking powder, salt, cinnamon, nutmeg, allspice and sugar.

Make a well in the centre of the dry ingredients and add oil, pumpkin puree, vanilla and rice milk. Slowly incorporate wet ingredients into dry ingredients. Sift in coconut flour and stir just until incorporated.

Spoon muffin batter into prepared muffin cups and sprinkle with topping. Bake 25 minutes or until toothpick in centre comes out clean. Cool completely before serving.

Makes 12 Muffins

Baked Donuts

Baked donuts are quick and easy, and better for you than fried donuts. Look for a donut pan in your favorite kitchen store.

Donut
½ cup rice milk
½ tsp. apple cider vinegar
¾ cups gluten free flour mix (*page 6*)
¼ tsp. xanthan gum or guar gum
¼ tsp. baking soda
1 tsp. baking powder
⅛ tsp. sea salt
2 tbsp. coconut sugar
⅛ tsp. nutmeg
⅛ tsp. cinnamon
¼ cup safflower oil or melted coconut oil
¼ cup unsweetened applesauce
1 tsp. vanilla extract
2 tbsp. coconut flour

Coconut Topping

¼ cup shredded coconut
1 tbsp. raw agave syrup

Preheat oven to 375°F.

In a measuring cup, combine rice milk and vinegar and set aside.

In a large bowl, add gluten free flour, xanthan gum, baking soda, baking powder, salt, sugar, nutmeg and cinnamon.

Make a well in the centre of the dry ingredients and add oil, applesauce, vanilla and rice milk. Slowly incorporate wet ingredients into dry ingredients. Sift in coconut flour and stir just until incorporated.

Spoon batter into donut pan and bake 15 minutes or until toothpick in centre comes out clean. Cool completely.

Brush cooled donuts with agave syrup and dip into coconut.

Makes 6 Donuts

Maple Pecan Granola Bars

Oats themselves are gluten free and are considered safe for most people with a gluten intolerance. However, oats can easily be contaminated with wheat, either during harvest, storage, or at other stages of processing. If you have a true gluten allergy, look for oats that are certified gluten-free.

1 ½ cups old fashioned oats (*not instant*), divided
2 tbsp. coconut sugar
1 cup shredded unsweetened coconut
⅓ cup hemp seeds
⅓ cup pecans, chopped
¼ cup coconut oil, melted
¼ cup maple syrup
1 tsp. pure maple extract
Pinch of sea salt
1 tsp. cinnamon

Preheat oven to 325°F.
Line a small baking sheet with parchment paper.

In a food processor, process 1 cup of oats and coconut sugar into a flour. Empty into a large bowl and add remaining ½ cup oats and all other ingredients. Mix well.

Press mixture firmly on prepared baking sheet. Using the sides of the parchment paper, shape into a rectangle (1-inch thickness). With a knife, cut into 12 bars.

Bake 35 minutes, until the edges are lightly browned.
Cool completely.

Makes 12 Bars

Oatmeal Raisin Cookies

Oatmeal cookies are a classic comfort food and high-fibre snack.

If you have a true gluten allergy look for oats that are certified gluten-free.

1 ¾ cups old fashioned oats, (*not instant*) divided
Pinch of sea salt
½ tsp. baking soda
1 tsp. cinnamon
⅓ cup coconut oil, softened
¼ cup honey
1 tsp. vanilla extract
¼ cup shredded unsweetened coconut
⅓ cup raisins
½ cup walnuts, chopped

Preheat oven to 350°F.
Line a small baking sheet with parchment paper.

In a food processor, process 1 cup of oats, sea salt, baking soda and cinnamon into a flour and set aside.

In a large bowl, cream together coconut oil, honey and vanilla.

Add oat flour and remaining ¾ cup oats, coconut, raisins and walnuts. Mix until all ingredients are combined. Scoop batter, ¼ cup at a time, on to prepared baking sheet and flatten to ½-inch thickness.

For soft, chewy cookies bake 15-18 minutes, until the edges are lightly browned. For firm, crisp cookies bake 18-20 minutes. Cool completely.

Makes 8-10 Cookies

Superfood Trail Mix

Create your own mix using your favorite nuts, seeds and other superfoods such as mulberries, cocoa nibs, golden berries or jungle peanuts...the combinations are endless.

½ cup unsweetened coconut flakes
½ cup raw pumpkin seeds
½ cup raw sunflower seeds
¼ cup dried cranberries or blueberries
¼ cup cacao beans, crushed

½ cup goji berries
½ cup hemp seeds
½ cup raisins
½ cup raw almonds

Mix all ingredients in a large container and enjoy.

Makes 4 cups

Breakfast Parfait

A lovely raw breakfast, snack or dessert. This delicious trail mix is topped with raw cashew cream supplying just the right amount of indulgence, without the guilt.

1 cup raw cashews, soaked overnight and drained
¼ cup almond milk (*page 7*)
1-2 tbsp. raw agave syrup
½ tsp. vanilla extract
½ cup superfood trail mix (*see recipe above*)

In a food processor, add cashews, milk, agave syrup and vanilla.

Process until smooth and creamy. Add more milk as needed until mixture reaches yogurt-like consistency.

Build your parfait by layering trail mix and cashew cream. Top with fresh fruit and serve.

*Cashew cream can be stored in refrigerator up to 3 days.

Makes 2 Servings

Coconut Balls

A lovely breakfast or snack made with the goodness of coconut.

¾ cup shredded, unsweetened coconut, divided
2 tsp. raw agave syrup
6 tbsp. almond butter
2 tsp. cocoa powder
1 tsp. vanilla extract or vanilla powder

Set ¼ cup shredded coconut aside to use as coating.

Place remaining ingredients into food processor and process until mixture comes together.

Take a small amount of mixture (about 1 tbsp.) and roll into a ball, then roll through reserved coconut.

Continue with remaining mixture and serve.

Makes 12 Balls

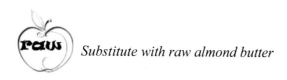 *Substitute with raw almond butter*

Spirulina Balls

These treats contain spirulina, an important source of nutrients and a high-quality vegan protein.

⅔ cup almonds
⅓ cup dates, pitted and chopped
⅔ cup brown rice cereal
2 tbsp. raw agave syrup
1 tbsp. spirulina powder
⅓ cup raisins
⅓ cup almond butter

Chop almonds and reserve ¼ of chopped almonds for garnish.

Place remaining chopped almonds, dates, cereal, agave syrup, spirulina, raisins and almond butter into a food processor.

Process until mixture forms into a ball.

Take a small amount of mixture (about 1 tbsp.) and roll into a ball, then roll through reserved almonds.

Continue with remaining mixture and serve.

Makes 12 Balls

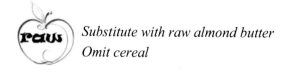

Substitute with raw almond butter
Omit cereal

VEGETABLE

&

SIDE DISHES

Veggie Wraps

These wraps make a healthy and attractive snack or party food.

NORI WRAPS

Rice
1 cup short grain brown rice
1 tbsp. Bragg liquid soy seasoning

Filling Options
Avocado
Cucumber
Carrots
Sesame seeds
Sprouts

Steam rice with 1 ¼ cups water and soy seasoning for 40 minutes. Cool slightly.

Take one sheet of nori and cut it in half. Place half sheet of nori horizontally on a sushi mat or piece of parchment paper and place about one tablespoon of rice along the left side of the nori sheet. Add filling ingredients vertically.

Take bottom left corner of nori and bring it up to the top center of the nori sheet. Tuck and roll to the right until you have a cone shape.

To keep the cone together, take one grain of cooked rice and squash it into the corner. This will stick the end down, holding the nori in position.

RICE PAPER WRAPS
10 rice paper rounds*

Fill a large shallow bowl with warm water. Place 1-2 sheets of rice paper in the water and soak for 30 seconds or until softened.

Remove softened rice paper from water and place on paper towel. Add your favorite fillings across the centre, leaving about 1" on either side.
Fold in the sides then tightly roll to enclose the filling. Repeat with remaining rolls.

*Rice paper can be found in most grocery stores

Breaded Eggplant

A delicious baked eggplant dish paired with a crunchy gluten-free bread crumb coating.

Eggplant
1 large eggplant
1 cup gluten free bread crumbs (*page 10*)
½ tsp. dried oregano
½ tsp. dried parsley
Pinch of sea salt
Pinch of pepper
½ cup tomato sauce
Fresh parsley

Tahini Sauce
2 tbsp. tahini
2 tbsp. water
1 tbsp. lemon juice

Slice eggplant into 1/4-inch round slices and sprinkle with sea salt. Let eggplant slices sit for 30 minutes. Rinse to remove salt and pat dry.

Preheat oven to 450°F.

Prepare the breading in a shallow dish by combining bread crumbs, oregano parsley, salt and pepper. Set aside.

In a second shallow dish, prepare the tahini sauce by mixing together tahini, water and lemon juice until smooth.

Brush eggplant on both sides with tahini mixture and then dip into bread crumb mixture. Make sure to coat both sides.

Place slices onto ungreased baking sheet and bake 10-15 minutes.

Turn slices over and top with tomato sauce. Bake an additional 10 minutes. Serve garnished with chopped parsley.

Serves 2-4

Baked Onion Rings

Everyone loves a side of onion rings, and this oven-baked version is simple and delicious.

Onion
2 large sweet onions

Breading
1 cup gluten-free bread crumbs
2 tbsp. sesame seeds

Batter
⅔ cup gluten-free flour mix (*page 6*)
¾ cup vegetable broth

Preheat oven to 425°F.
Grease 2 baking sheets with coconut oil.

Slice onions into 1/4-inch slices and separate into rings, keeping only large, whole rings (*reserve remaining slices for other dishes*).

In a shallow dish, prepare breading by combining bread crumbs and sesame seeds.

In another shallow dish, prepare batter by whisking together flour and vegetable broth until smooth.

Dip onion rings into broth mixture and transfer to bread crumb mixture. Make sure to coat both sides.

Place rings onto prepared baking sheets.

Bake 15 minutes per side, or until coating is crisp.

Serves 2-4

Tomato Sauce

Transform a can of tomatoes into a flavorful sauce for pasta simply by adding garlic and a few spices.

2 tbsp. extra virgin olive oil
1 onion, finely chopped
2 cloves garlic, finely chopped
2 carrots, peeled and grated
1 zucchini, grated
2 (680g) jar of strained tomatoes or 2 (800ml) cans diced tomatoes*
½ cup water
handful of basil leaves, finely chopped
1-2 tsp. dried Italian seasonings (*oregano, basil, marjoram etc.*)
Sea salt and pepper

In a sauté pan, heat olive oil on medium heat. Add garlic and onion and sauté until garlic is fragrant.

Pour cooked onions and remaining ingredients in slow cooker and cook over low heat for 7-8 hours.

Sauce can be used immediately or divide into smaller portions and refrigerated or frozen.

* *if using canned tomatoes omit 1/2 cup water*

Serves 6-8

Pizza Sauce

Add the following ingredients in to the above sauce recipe:

1 tbsp. balsamic vinegar
1 tbsp. coconut sugar
2-3 fresh basil leaves

Serves 6-8

Roasted Red Peppers

Roasted red peppers store well, in either the refrigerator or freezer, and provide a quick and easy way to spice up a favorite recipe.

4-5 red peppers, cut into quarters, stems and seeds removed

Move the oven rack to the top position and preheat the oven to broil. Line a baking sheet with foil.

Lay the peppers flat on prepared baking sheet, skin side up. Press flat with your hand.

Broil 10-15 minutes, or until the skins are black, but the flesh underneath is still soft and moist.

Once the skins have blackened, remove peppers from the oven and place in a large paper bag, or sealable container. Allow peppers to steam for at least 10 minutes.

After the peppers have had time to steam, remove from paper bag and gently pull blackened skins off.

Roasted peppers can either be stored in the refrigerator or frozen between sheets of waxed paper in an airtight container.

To store in fridge, slice roasted peppers into thin strips and place in a jar with a tight-fitting lid. Fill jar with just enough olive oil to cover pepper strips and seal tightly.

Roasted Red Pepper Sauce

Puree 1 roasted red pepper and add into Tomato Sauce (opposite page).

Basmati Rice Crackers

Making your own whole grain crackers is easy and a great way to use up leftover brown rice!

2 cups cooked brown basmati rice
¼ cup extra virgin olive oil
1 ¾ cups gluten-free flour mix (*page 6*)
¼ cup sesame seeds
1 tsp. baking soda
1 tsp. sea salt
½ cup warm water

Preheat the oven to 375°F.
Line baking sheet with parchment paper.

Process the cooked rice and oil in a food processor for 1 minute. Add in flour, sesame seeds, baking soda and salt and process again. Slowly incorporate enough water to form a dough that comes together in to a ball.

Transfer mixture onto a large sheet of parchment paper. Cover with an additional sheet of parchment paper.

Using a rolling pin, roll dough out into a large rectangle, to about 1/4-inch thickness.

Remove top sheet of parchment paper and cut dough into squares and place on prepared baking sheet. With the ends of the fork, poke holes into crackers.

Bake on middle rack for 30 minutes.
Remove from oven and flip crackers over. Let crackers rest 20 minutes or more before returning to the oven to bake for an additional 25 minutes.

Cool completely and store in airtight container.

Makes 5-6 Dozen Crackers

Flax Bread

Checking the internal temperature of bread is a foolproof way to tell if it is fully baked. An instant-read thermometer through the side of the loaf should read 200°F.

3 flax egg replacements (*page 7*)
1 pkg. instant yeast (*approx 2 ½ tsp.*)
2 tbsp. coconut sugar
1 cup warm water or milk (*around 100F*)
3 cups gluten-free flour mix (*page 6*)
2 tsp. xanthan gum or guar gum
1 tsp. sea salt
2 tbsp. extra virgin olive oil

Prepare flax egg replacement and let cool before using.

In a small bowl, dissolve yeast and sugar in warm water for 5 minutes until frothy.

In a large bowl, combine flour, guar gum and salt. Make a well in the centre of the dry ingredients and add yeast mixture, egg replacement and oil. Stir well to combine. Knead with hands just until all the flour has been incorporated. Add additional flour as needed until dough is no longer sticky.

Brush bowl and dough with olive oil. Cover bowl and let dough rest 45 minutes in a warm place.

Preheat oven to 400°F.

Transfer dough into a greased loaf pan. Brush top of bread with olive oil and sprinkle with sesame seeds or flax seeds.
Bake 50-60 minutes. Test for doneness by tapping the bottom of the bread loaf and listening for hollow sound or until internal temperature reaches 200°F.

Best served warm or lightly toasted   Makes 1 Loaf

Buns

Once dough has risen, shape dough into 10 balls and place on greased baking sheet. Cover and let rise 15 additional minutes. Bake 25-30 minutes at 400°F.

Best served warm or lightly toasted.   Makes 10 Buns

Lentil Hummus

This hummus dip is similar to the traditional hummus made with chickpeas, but is much easier to digest.

¾ cup red lentils, rinsed
½ tsp. sea salt
¼ cup tahini (*sesame butter*)
1-2 garlic cloves, minced
¼ cup chopped roasted red pepper (*page 37*)
3 tbsp. extra virgin olive oil
Juice of ½ lemon (*or more to taste*)
Pinch sweet paprika
1 ½ tbsp. minced parsley

Place lentils in a pot and cover with 2 cups water. Boil, then reduce heat and simmer gently for 15 minutes until tender. Once cooked, remove from heat and cool. Drain excess water.

Combine cooled lentils, salt, tahini, garlic, red pepper, olive oil and lemon juice in a food processor and blend until smooth and creamy.

Garnish with paprika and parsley.

Serves 2-4

MAIN DISHES

Shepherd's Pie

Shepherd's pie is pure comfort food, and this vegan version will satisfy the taste buds in any crowd.

3 large sweet potatoes, peeled
⅓ cup green lentils (*approx. 1 cup cooked lentils*)
1 tbsp. extra virgin olive oil
1 onion, finely chopped
1 garlic clove, minced
¼ cup vegetable broth
1 cup chopped vegetables (*carrots, celery, zucchini, etc.*)
½ cup fresh or frozen peas
½ cup fresh or frozen organic corn
1 tbsp. vegan Worcestershire sauce
½ tbsp. Bragg liquid soy seasoning
Sea salt and pepper

Steam whole sweet potatoes for 20 minutes, until cooked through.

Simmer lentils in 2 cups water or broth for 20 minutes. Strain and set aside.

Preheat oven to 375°F.
Line a loaf pan with parchment paper.

In a large frying pan, sauté onion and garlic in olive oil until fragrant. Add vegetable broth, chopped vegetables, peas and corn and cook 3-4 minutes. Add Worcestershire sauce, soy seasoning and cooked lentils.

Mash cooked sweet potatoes.
Add ½ cup of mashed sweet potato to the lentil mixture to help with binding. Reserve the remaining sweet potato.

Pour lentil mixture into prepared loaf pan.
Season remaining sweet potato with salt and pepper to taste and spoon over lentil mixture. Bake 35-40 minutes uncovered.

Serves 2-4

Detox Soup

In Traditional Chinese Medicine and Indian Ayurveda, green mung beans are frequently recommended for detoxifying the body.

8 cups vegetable broth
¼ cup mung beans
¼ cup quinoa, soaked and drained
1 cup diced celery
1 cup diced carrots
1 cup chopped green beans
1 clove garlic, minced
2 cups chopped baby spinach or kale
½ cup chopped parsley

Bring broth to a boil in a large pot. Reduce heat to low and simmer mung beans, covered, for 45 minutes.

Add quinoa, celery, carrots, green beans and garlic and bring back to boil. Lower heat and simmer an additional 15 minutes.

Remove from heat and add spinach leaves and parsley before serving.

Use it as a meal anytime you wish to add support to your overall detoxing or cleansing program.

Serves 2-4

Mung beans are small, green, pellet-like beans, which can be found among other dried beans in your bulk food store and grocery stores. They need no pre-soaking and are easy to digest.

Spaghetti Squash

Spaghetti squash makes a good side dish, but you can also use it as a pasta substitute for your main course.

1 small spaghetti squash (*approx. 1 lb.*)
3-4 tbsp. extra virgin olive oil
1 clove garlic, crushed
1 shallot or small onion, chopped
½ lb. mushrooms, sliced (*approx. 2 cups*)
1 tbsp. Bragg liquid soy seasoning
¼ cup vegetable broth
1 cup chopped greens (*spinach, rapini, collards, swiss chard, etc.*)

Preheat oven to 375°F.

Thoroughly wash squash to remove any debris.
Cut squash in half length-wise and place in a shallow baking pan, cut side down. Bake for 40 minutes or until knife can easily pierce through the squash.

Alternatively, you can bake the squash whole. Pierce the squash several times to allow steam to escape and then bake for 1 hour.

Meanwhile, in a large skillet over medium heat, add oil, garlic and onions and cook until onions become translucent.
Add mushrooms and soy sauce. Cook 2-3 minutes to release water from the mushrooms.
Add vegetable broth and chopped greens.

Cook an additional 3-4 minutes until greens have wilted. Add additional broth if needed to help with cooking process.

Remove squash from oven and remove any seeds. Use a fork to separate out the spaghetti strands.

Serve topped with mushroom mixture.

Serves 2-4

Quinoa Tomato Soup

This soup is hearty and healthy with quinoa and lots of veggies.

1 tbsp. extra virgin olive oil
1 medium onion, diced
2 cloves garlic, minced
2 carrots, peeled and chopped
2 celery stalks, chopped
1 cup chopped zucchini
½ cup fresh green beans, cut into ¾" pieces
1-2 small beets, peeled and cubed
4 cups vegetable broth
1 can crushed or diced tomatoes (398ml)
2 bay leaves
1 tsp. dried thyme
1 tsp. dried parsley
¼ cup quinoa, soaked and drained
Sea salt and pepper

Heat the olive oil in large, heavy-bottomed stockpot over medium-low heat. Once hot, add the onion and garlic and cook until tender, approximately 5 minutes.

Add the chopped vegetables, vegetable broth, tomatoes, bay leaves, thyme and parsley. Reduce the heat to low, cover and cook 15 minutes.

Add quinoa and continue to cook an addition 20 minutes. Season with salt and pepper to taste.

Remove bay leaves and serve.

Serves 2-4

Sweet Potato Gnocchi

Gnocchi are Italian dumplings traditionally made from potato and flour. Sweet potato gives a delicious twist to this classic recipe.

½ lb. sweet potatoes (*approx. 2-3 small*), cooked and cooled
¼ tsp. sea salt
1 cup gluten-free flour mix (*page 6*)
1 cup roasted red pepper sauce (*page 36*) or prepared pasta sauce

Grate the sweet potato (or use a ricer) and place in a large bowl. Sprinkle in salt and ½ cup flour at a time and combine until you have formed a dough that is moist but not sticky.

Divide dough into 4 sections and gently roll each section into a log about 1" thick. Use a knife to cut logs into 1" pieces. Dust with a bit more flour.

Holding a fork, gently roll gnocchi pieces down fork tines, pressing with your thumb, to make ridges on each piece. Set aside, dusting with a bit more flour if needed, until you are ready to boil them.

Meanwhile, heat tomato sauce in a small pot over low heat.

Bring a large pot of salted water to a boil.

Cook the gnocchi in batches by dropping them, roughly 20 at a time, into the boiling water for about 5 minutes or until they begin to float on the surface.

Remove with a slotted spoon and add to sauce.
Repeat with remaining gnocchi and serve.

Serves 2 to 4

Fried Quinoa

Cooked quinoa replaces rice in this twist on Chinese fried rice. The quinoa can be cooked well in advance and added at the last minute.

2 tsp. sesame oil
1 tbsp. extra virgin olive oil
1 garlic clove, crushed or chopped
½ onion, diced
2 tbsp. chopped ginger
1 cup mushrooms, thinly sliced
2-3 tsp. Bragg liquid soy seasoning
1 cup vegetables (*snow peas, broccoli, carrots, red peppers, etc.*)
½ cup fresh or frozen peas
¼ cup vegetable broth or water
½ cup cooked quinoa (*page 55*)
2 green onions, chopped
Sesame seeds as garnish

In nonstick wok or large nonstick frying pan, heat oils and garlic over medium-low heat. Add onion and ginger and sauté 5 to 6 minutes or until softened.

Add mushrooms and soy seasoning. Increase heat to medium-high and cook 4-6 minutes or until mushrooms are tender. Add in vegetables and peas and cook another 3-4 minutes, until vegetables are tender crisp, using broth as needed to help with the cooking process.

Add quinoa and cook until heated through, about 2 minutes.

Serve garnished with green onions and sesame seeds.

Serves 2-4

How to Cook Quinoa

Quinoa is often thought of as a grain but is, in fact, a seed. Quinoa should be soaked and rinsed thoroughly to remove the bitter resin (called saponin) that coats the seeds.

Soak 1 cup quinoa in cold water for 5 minutes and then strain.

In saucepan, bring 2 cups water and quinoa to a boil. Reduce heat to low and simmer, covered, for 15 minutes. Remove from heat and let stand for 5 minutes. Fluff with a fork and serve.

Serves 2-4

Slow Cooker Lentils

A hearty slow cooker meal that is simple to make and satisfying for any meal of the day.

1 sweet potato, peeled and cubed
2 carrots, peeled and chopped
1 onion, chopped
2 stalks celery, chopped
¾ cup green lentils
¼ cup red lentils
1 clove garlic, minced
1 cup tomato puree
4 cups vegetable broth
⅛ tsp. cayenne pepper (*or more to taste*)
½ tsp. cumin
¼ tsp. nutmeg

Place all ingredients in slow cooker.

Cover and set on low for 8-10 hours or on high for 4 hours.

Serves 2-4

Meatless Meatballs

These meatballs are delicious atop your favorite pasta. Make them any night of the week and you'll look forward to the leftovers!

1 flax egg replacement (*page 7*)
1-2 tbsp. extra virgin olive oil
½ onion, chopped
2 cups chopped mushrooms (*approx. ½ lb.*)
¼ tsp. sea salt
½ cup walnuts
½ cup gluten-free bread crumbs (*page 10*)
¼ cup chopped parsley
1 garlic clove, minced
½ lb. gluten-free spaghetti
1 cup tomato sauce (*page 36*) or prepared pasta sauce

Prepare flax egg replacement and set aside.
Preheat oven to 375°F.

Heat oil over medium heat in a large frying pan. Add onion, mushrooms and salt and cook 5 minutes, until mushrooms are tender and their juices are released.

In a food processor, add walnuts and process until fine. Add in cooked mushrooms and their juices, flax egg, bread crumbs, parsley and garlic. Process again until the mixture holds together when rolled into a ball.

Roll out 20 balls and place on parchment-lined baking sheet.

Bake for 35-40 minutes, turning balls half way through. Remove from oven when crispy on all sides.

Meanwhile, prepare spaghetti according to package directions and heat pasta sauce over low heat.

Drain spaghetti when cooked and divide among 4 serving dishes, top each with 5 to 6 meatballs and a ladleful of sauce.

Serves 4

Pizza

Top this gluten-free pizza crust with your favorite toppings and enjoy pizza night again!

2 flax egg replacement (*page 7*)
1 pkg. instant yeast (*approx. 2 ½ tsp.*)
1 tbsp. coconut sugar
1 cup warm water (around 100°F)
3 cups gluten-free flour mix (*page 6*)
2 tsp. xanthan gum or guar gum
1 tsp. sea salt
2 tbsp. extra virgin olive oil
1 cup pizza sauce (*page 36*) or prepared pizza sauce
Toppings of choice (*olives, peppers, onions, mushrooms, etc.*)
Vegan Cheese (*optional*)

Prepare flax egg replacement and set aside.

In a small bowl, dissolve yeast and sugar in warm water for 5 minutes until frothy.

In a large bowl, combine flour, guar gum and salt. Make a well in the centre of the dry ingredients and add yeast mixture, flax egg and olive oil. Stir well to combine. Knead dough until all the flour has been incorporated. Rub dough with olive oil. Cover bowl and let rise 35-40 minutes.

Preheat oven to 400°F. Dust pizza pan or baking sheet with flour.

Remove dough from bowl and gently place into pizza pan. Gently roll out dough with rolling pin to 3/4" thickness.

Cover with sauce and toppings. Bake 25-30 minutes.

Makes 1 Large Pizza

Veggie Burgers

These veggie burgers get their rich, earthy flavor from mushrooms and pecans.

3-4 tbsp. extra virgin olive oil
½ onion, chopped
2 garlic cloves, chopped
1 lb. mushrooms, sliced (*approx. 4 cups*)
2 tbsp. Bragg liquid soy seasoning
2 cups baby spinach
½ cup chopped parsley
½ cup gluten-free bread crumbs (*page 10*)
½ cup ground pecans

In a sauté pan, heat oil and sauté garlic and onion over medium heat for about 2-3 minutes. Add mushrooms and soy seasoning and cook an additional 2-3 minutes or until mushrooms are tender.

Remove from heat and add spinach.

Cool mixture 5-10 minutes before transferring to food processor along with parsley, bread crumbs and pecans. Process until mixture holds together when gathered into a ball.

Shape into 8 patties and refrigerate 30 minutes.

Preheat oven to 375°F and bake on parchment lined baking sheet for 12-15 minutes.

Patties can also be grilled 5-6 minutes per side until they get nice and crispy on the outside.

Serve on gluten-free buns (*page 41*) and baked onion rings (*page 34*).

Serves 4-8

Thai Pumpkin Soup

Thai pumpkin soup is the perfect soup to warm you up, especially in the fall, when pumpkins are plenty.

1 tbsp. extra virgin olive oil
3 cloves garlic, minced
1 small piece ginger, peeled
2 shallots or ½ onion, chopped
2 tsp. Thai red curry paste *(page 13)*
2 cups pumpkin puree or canned pumpkin (*not pumpkin pie filling*)
2 cups vegetable broth
2 stalks lemon grass or zest from 1 lemon
½ cup canned coconut milk
Minced cilantro or Thai basil for garnish

In a large pot, heat oil over medium-low heat. Add garlic, ginger and shallots and stir, cooking just until softened.

Add curry paste and stir until fragrant.
Add pumpkin puree, vegetable broth and lemon grass.

Simmer on low heat for 15 minutes.
Serve as is, or puree in a blender for a smooth soup.

Serve garnished with coconut milk and cilantro.

Serves 2-4

Homemade Pumpkin Puree

Wash and cut pumpkin (*or any other winter squash*) in half.
Remove seeds and any stringy strands. Bake, face down in 400°F oven for 30 minutes or until fork can easily pierce through the flesh.

Cool, remove pumpkin pulp and place in a food processor.
Process until you have a smooth puree.

Leftover puree can be frozen for up to 1 year.

Thai Squash

Using prepared red curry paste is an easy and fast way to add traditional Thai flavors to this meal.

1 tbsp. extra virgin olive oil
1 onion, chopped
1 red pepper, seeds and ribs removed and cut into 1/4-inch strips
2 garlic cloves, finely chopped
1 tbsp. peeled and finely chopped fresh ginger
1 tbsp. Thai red curry paste (*page 13*)
1 cup canned coconut milk (*full fat or low fat*)
1 tbsp. Bragg liquid soy seasoning
2 cups peeled and cubed acorn squash
1 cup chopped vegetables (*peppers, carrots, zucchini etc.*)
4 green onions, chopped (*reserve tops for garnish*)
Cooked quinoa (*page 55*), brown rice or Thai noodles
Thai basil, chopped

Heat olive oil in a large frying pan over medium heat. Add onion and cook, stirring occasionally, until the onion has softened, about 6 minutes.

Add peppers, garlic, ginger and curry paste. Stir to combine, and cook until fragrant, about 1 minute.

Add the coconut milk, soy seasoning, squash, vegetables and green onions and bring to a simmer, stirring occasionally, until the squash is fork-tender but still firm, about 15-20 minutes.

Serve over cooked quinoa, rice or noodles.

Garnish with basil and green onion tops.

Serves 2-4

Chickpea Curry

Serve this tasty dish over your favorite brown rice or noodles.

2 tbsp. extra virgin olive oil
½ onion, chopped
2 garlic cloves, crushed
1 tbsp. Thai yellow or green curry paste (*page 13*)
⅛ cup vegetable broth
2 carrots, peeled and sliced
1 cup broccoli, chopped
½ cup sliced green or red peppers
1 (15oz.) can organic chickpeas
½ cup canned coconut milk
½ tbsp. Bragg liquid soy seasoning
4 green onions, chopped
Handful cilantro, chopped
Cooked quinoa (*page 55*), brown rice or Thai noodles

Heat oil in a large frying pan over medium heat along with onion and garlic. Sauté until onions have softened. Add curry paste and cook until fragrant.

Add remaining ingredients and simmer 10-15 minutes.

Serve over quinoa, brown rice or noodles and garnish with chopped green onion and cilantro.

Serves 2-4

Tex-Mex Quinoa

Loaded with lots of protein, fibre and colorful vegetables, this is a perfect side dish or weekday lunch.

¾ cup quinoa
1 tbsp. extra virgin olive oil
1 onion, chopped
1 garlic clove, minced
1 ½ cups vegetable broth
½ tsp. cumin
⅛ tsp. cayenne pepper
½ cup fresh or frozen organic corn
1 carrot, peeled and diced
1 (15oz.) can black beans, rinsed and drained
½ cup prepared salsa
Parsley or cilantro, chopped

Soak quinoa in water for 5 minutes, drain and rinse.

Heat oil in a large frying pan with onion and garlic. Cook until fragrant and onions have softened.

Add broth and quinoa and bring to a boil. Reduce heat and simmer 10 minutes.

Add cumin, cayenne, corn, carrot, black beans and salsa. Simmer an additional 5-10 minutes until all liquid has been absorbed.

Serve garnished with freshly chopped cilantro or parsley.

Serves 4-6

Baked Wild Rice

This foolproof rice dish cooks to the perfect texture every time.

2 ½ cups vegetable broth
1 bay leaf
2 tbsp. extra virgin olive oil
½ onion, chopped
1 cup sliced mushrooms
1 tbsp. Bragg liquid soy seasoning
¾ cup short grain brown rice
¼ cup wild rice
¼ cup fresh, frozen or dried cranberries
½ cup pecans, toasted and coarsely chopped—*optional*
Chopped parsley to garnish

Preheat oven to 375°F.

In a saucepan, bring vegetable broth and bay leaf to a simmer.

Meanwhile, heat oil in a skillet over medium heat. Add onion and sauté 2-3 minutes. Add mushrooms and soy seasoning and continue to cook an additional 2-3 minutes.

Add brown rice, wild rice and cranberries to skillet and stir until all the grains are well coated.

Transfer rice to a loaf pan or casserole dish. Pour heated broth overtop rice. Cover and carefully transfer to pre-heated oven.

Bake 50-60 minutes or until all liquid has been absorbed.

Remove from oven and discard bay leaf.

Serve topped with crushed pecans and parsley.

Serves 2-4

Baked Wild Rice
served in oven baked squash bowls

Desserts

Vanilla Cheesecake

This is an amazing vegan "cheesecake" that is very rich, decadent and delicious!

Crust
¾ cup walnuts
¼ cup shredded unsweetened coconut
Pinch of sea salt
1 tbsp. cocoa powder
2 tbsp. raw agave syrup
½ tsp. vanilla extract

In a food processor, process all ingredients until mixture holds together. Add water if needed to help it stay together.

Press into bottom of 6" round springform pan. Place in freezer while preparing filling.

Filling
30g cocoa butter *(page 9)*
2 cups cashews or macadamia nuts, soaked overnight and drained
½ cup raw agave syrup
1 tbsp. lemon juice
1 tbsp. vanilla extract

Melt cocoa butter over a double boiler.

Place melted cocoa butter, cashews agave syrup, lemon and vanilla into food processor and process until smooth and creamy. Pour over prepared crust.

Freeze for 1 hour or until set.
Once set, cheesecake can decorated with your favorite fruits and refrigerated for up to 1 week.

Substitute with raw cocoa powder
Melt cocoa butter in a dehydrator

Homemade Chocolate

Homemade chocolates are incredibly easy to make and delicious.

40g cocoa butter—approx. ⅓ cup finely chopped (*page 9*)
6 tbsp. cocoa powder
2 tbsp. raw agave syrup
Pinch of sea salt
1 tsp. vanilla extract or powder

Melt cocoa butter over a double boiler. Once melted, combine all ingredients in a bowl and stir until smooth.

Pour into chocolate molds or onto a baking sheet lined with parchment paper and refrigerate.
Once firm, remove from molds and store in the refrigerator.

 Substitute with raw cocoa powder
Melt cocoa butter in a dehydrator

Coconut Bites

These raw food bites make a wonderful snack any time of day.

¾ cup unsweetened coconut flakes, divided
16 medjool dates*, pitted
16 pecan halves

Set aside ¼ cup coconut flakes for garnish.

In a food processor, combine ½ cup coconut and dates.

Process several minutes until smooth and gathers into a ball. With your hands, shape into 16 balls.

Roll each ball into reserved coconut flakes.
Flatten slightly and garnish with pecan half.

Makes 16 Treats

* *if using cooking dates, you may need to rehydrate them in water before using.*

Avocado Pudding

With avocados and a few other ingredients, you can have healthy, delicious vegan pudding in minutes!

¼ cup cashews (*or any other nut or seed of choice*)
2 medium avocados, mashed
¼ cup cocoa powder
¼ cup raw agave syrup
½ cup rice milk or almond milk
1 tsp. vanilla extract
Pinch of sea salt

In a coffee grinder, process cashews until fine.

Place ground cashews and remaining ingredients in a food processor and process until smooth and creamy.

Spoon into dessert dishes.

Best served chilled.

Makes 2-4 servings

Substitute with raw cocoa powder and homemade almond milk (page 7)

Chocolate Cupcakes

Avocado replaces the egg in this rich, moist cupcake, which is topped with a delicious avocado frosting.

1 cup rice milk
1 tsp. apple cider vinegar
1 ½ cups gluten-free flour mix (*page 6*)
½ tsp. xanthan gum or guar gum
½ tsp. baking soda
1 ½ tsp. baking powder
⅛ tsp. sea salt
¼ cup coconut sugar
2 tbsp. carob powder or cocoa powder
½ cup coconut oil, melted
⅓ cup mashed avocado
1 tsp. vanilla extract
2 tbsp. coconut flour

Avocado frosting

1 avocado
2 tbsp. agave syrup
1 tsp. vanilla extra
2 tbsp. cocoa powder

Puree all ingredients in a blender or food processor. Spoon into a piping bag.

Preheat oven to 375°F.
Line 12-cup muffin pan with paper liners.

In a measuring cup, combine rice milk and apple cider vinegar and set aside to curdle.

In a large bowl, add gluten-free flour mix, xanthan gum, baking soda, baking powder, salt, sugar and carob powder.

Make a well in the centre of dry ingredients and add oil, avocado, vanilla and rice milk mixture. Slowly incorporate wet ingredients into dry ingredients.
Sift in coconut flour and mix until well incorporated.

Spoon batter into prepared muffin cups.

Bake 20-25 minutes or until toothpick in centre comes out clean.
Cool completely before frosting.

Makes 12 Cupcakes

Sugar Cookies

A vegan cookie recipe that can be rolled out and cut into many wonderfully creative shapes.

½ tbsp. olive oil
1 tbsp. rice flour
1 tbsp. water
½ tsp. baking powder
⅓ cup coconut oil, softened
⅓ cup coconut sugar
1 tsp. vanilla extract
1 cup gluten-free flour mix (*page 6*)
⅛ tsp. xanthan gum or guar gum
½ tsp. baking powder
⅛ tsp. sea salt

In a small bowl, mix rice flour, water, oil and baking powder together and let rest 5 minutes.

Preheat oven to 375°F.
Line baking sheet with parchment paper.

In a large bowl, cream coconut oil and sugar using a hand mixer until light and fluffy. Add olive oil mixture and vanilla.

Sift in gluten-free flour, xanthan gum, baking powder and sea salt.

Knead into a soft dough.

Place dough between two sheets of parchment paper and roll out to desired thickness. Using your favorite cookie cutter, cut into desired shapes and place on prepared baking sheet.

Bake 8-10 minutes or until edges just start to brown.

Makes 18-24 Cookies

Coconut Almond Treats

The combination of coconut, chocolate and almonds makes for a wonderfully rich treat.

⅓ cup canned coconut milk
¼ cup coconut oil
⅛ cup agave syrup
1 ½ cups shredded, unsweetened coconut
12 whole almonds
4-5 oz. baking chocolate or homemade chocolate (*page 76*)

In a medium-sized pan, heat coconut milk, coconut oil and agave syrup, just until oil has melted.

Remove from heat, add shredded coconut and mix well.

Shape mixture into 12 tightly packed mounds and top with whole almond. Place on a baking sheet lined with parchment paper.

Freeze for 30 minutes.

Meanwhile, melt chocolate over double boiler. Add 1 teaspoon of coconut oil, if needed, to thin out the chocolate.

Remove coconut mounds from freezer and place on wire rack. Drizzle chocolate overtop coconut mounds and return to parchment paper. Chill until set.

Makes 12 Treats

Fig Cookies

These cookies are reminiscent of the classic Fig Newton cookies.

Dough
½ cup coconut oil
½ cup coconut sugar
1 flax egg replacement (*page 7*)
2 tsp. vanilla extract
Pinch of sea salt
1 ¼ cups gluten-free flour (*page 6*)
1 tsp. xanthan gum or guar gum
2 tsp. baking powder

Filling
1 cup chopped dried figs*
¼ cup raisins
¼ cup applesauce

In a food processor add all ingredients and process until it becomes a smooth paste, scraping down sides as needed.

In a large bowl, cream coconut oil and sugar using a hand mixer. Add egg replacement, vanilla and salt.

Sift in flour, xanthan gum and baking powder. Knead until you have a smooth workable paste.

Divide dough into 4 sections. Set aside and prepare filling.

Preheat oven to 375°F.
Line baking sheet with parchment paper.

Between two sheets of parchment paper, roll out one section of dough into a 3x12" rectangle and approximately ¼" thickness. Add additional flour as needed to keep dough from sticking to the parchment paper.

Remove top layer of parchment paper. Spoon filling down the centre of rectangle. Using parchment paper as a guide, fold dough over the filling making sure to seal it. Flatten slightly. Remove parchment paper and cut into squares.

Place on prepared baking sheet. Repeat with remaining dough.
Bake 20-25 minutes or until lightly browned.

Makes 40 Cookies

* *make sure to remove the hard stem from the dried figs and soak in hot water for 15 minutes before chopping.*

Cocoa Carob Treats

Unlike chocolate, carob is high in calcium and potassium and is naturally caffeine free. If you aren't a fan of carob's uniquely nutty and malty flavour, I recommend replacing it with cocoa powder.

1 cup dates, chopped
2 cups walnuts
1 tbsp. coconut oil (*at room temperature*)
¼ cup cocoa powder
¼ cup carob powder
1 tsp. vanilla extract
1 oz. organic dark chocolate, melted-*optional*
1 oz. organic white chocolate, melted-*optional*

Place dates in a cup and add enough hot water to cover the dates completely. Let rest 10 minutes before straining.

In a food processor, combine dates, walnuts, coconut oil, cocoa powder, carob powder and vanilla extract. Process until mixture holds together when pressed into a ball.

Pour mixture onto a sheet of parchment paper and using the sides of the parchment paper shape into a square approx 1" thick.

Remove parchment paper and cut into 16 squares. Alternatively, pack the mixture into your favorite mold for a variety of fun shapes.

Place squares over a wire rack and decorate by drizzling melted chocolate over treats in a zigzag fashion.

Refrigerate until chocolate has set.

Makes 16 Squares

 Substitute with raw cocoa and raw carob powders
Soak dates 3-4 hours until softened

Cinnamon Bun Cookies

These cookies will fill your home with the wonderful scent of cinnamon and can be enjoyed without the guilt.

Dough

1 ¼ cups gluten free flour mix (*page 6*)
¼ tsp. xanthan gum or guar gum
2 tbsp. coconut sugar
½ tsp. cinnamon
2 tsp. baking powder
¼ tsp baking soda
⅛ tsp. sea salt
3 tbsp. coconut oil
¼ cup pumpkin puree
1 flax egg replacement (*page 7*)
¼ cup canned coconut milk
1 tsp. vanilla
Frosting-optional (*page 91*)

Filling

½ cup pecans
¼ cup coconut sugar
½ tsp. cinnamon
¼ tsp. nutmeg
¼ tsp. allspice
½ cup canned or homemade pumpkin puree (*page 64*)

Prepare filling by placing pecans, sugar and spices in a food processor and process until fine. Add to pumpkin puree, mix well and set aside.

Sift flour, xanthan gum, sugar, cinnamon, baking powder, baking soda and salt into a large bowl. Blend in coconut oil until mixture resembles coarse crumbs.

In a smaller bowl, mix together pumpkin puree, flax egg, coconut milk and vanilla until well combined.

Add pumpkin mixture into flour mixture and combine to form a soft dough. Add additional flour as needed until dough is soft but not sticky.

Spread dough out onto a sheet of parchment paper. Cover with an additional sheet of parchment paper and roll dough out into a rectangle (*approx. 12"x 8"*).

Prepare filling as above and spread over dough, leaving 1" around edges. Carefully roll the dough into a log, starting at the short end, using parchment paper as a guide. Wrap log up with parchment paper and refrigerate 1 hour.

Preheat oven to 425°F.
Line baking sheet with parchment paper.

Remove dough from fridge, unwrap and cut into 1" slices.
Place on prepared baking sheet and bake 15-18 minutes until
bottoms are golden brown.
Cool cookies completely before frosting (*if desired*).

Frosting: Combine ¼ cup coconut oil, 2 tbsp. agave syrup and 1
tsp. ground cinnamon together into a smooth frosting.

Makes 20 Cookies

Coconut Macaroons

Whip up a batch of these addictive macaroons with just a few simple ingredients. Enjoy them plain or topped with dark chocolate.

⅓ cup gluten-free flour mix (*page 6*)
2 ½ cups unsweetened, finely shredded coconut
½ cup canned coconut milk
¼ cup raw agave syrup
Pinch of sea salt
1 tsp. vanilla extract
3 oz. dark chocolate—*optional*

Preheat oven to 350°F.
Line a baking sheet with parchment paper.

In a large bowl, add flour, coconut, coconut milk, agave syrup, salt and vanilla. Combine all of the ingredients until coconut is completely moist.

Form the mixture into firmly packed 1" balls (*a small ice cream scoop works well*) and place them on prepared baking sheets.

Bake 10-12 minutes or until lightly browned along edges.

Cool completely before drizzling with melted chocolate (*if desired*).

Makes 18–20 Macaroons

Sesame Seed Cookies

These cookies are rich in calcium and their nutty aroma and wholesome taste make them delicious any time of day.

1 ½ cups gluten-free flour mix (*page 6*)
½ tsp. baking soda
Pinch of sea salt
¼ cup tahini (*sesame butter*)
¼ cup safflower oil or coconut oil
⅓ cup agave syrup
½ cup sesame seeds

Preheat oven to 350°F.
Line baking sheet with parchment paper.

In a medium bowl, combine flour, baking soda and sea salt.
Make a well in the centre and add tahini, oil and agave syrup.

Slowly incorporate wet ingredients into dry ingredients until you have a smooth, slightly sticky dough.

Roll into 16 balls and then roll into sesame seeds.

Place on prepared baking sheet and flatten with your fingers.

Bake 12 minutes or until edges begin to brown.

Makes 16 Cookies

Honey Sesame Snaps

This delicious candy is made using just two simple ingredients.

⅔ cup honey
1 ½ cup white or brown sesame seeds
½ cup black sesame seeds*

In a small saucepan, heat honey over medium-low heat until temperature reaches 300°F on a candy thermometer.
(*If you don't have a candy thermometer, you can place a small amount of the simmering honey into very cold water, it will solidify and separates into hard brittle threads when it reaches the correct temperature.*)

When honey reaches the correct temperature, immediately remove from heat and add sesame seeds. Mix until all sesame seeds are coated with honey.

Pour onto prepared baking sheet. Cover with an additional sheet of parchment paper and roll out to desired thickness.

Refrigerate until set.

Once set, break the candy into pieces and serve.

Makes 20 Pieces

* Black sesame seeds can be found at grocery stores and Asian markets. If unable to find black sesame seeds, white or brown sesame seeds can be substituted.

Recipe Index

Recipe Index

Recipe Index

Recipe Index

About the Author

 Rita Mustafa, founder of Oasis Health & Wellness, is a Holistic Nutritionist and Registered Acupuncturist, specializing in custom treatments tailored to each individual's unique body chemistry.

In her practice, she utilizes the latest tools to assess the body's responses to ongoing environmental, dietary and emotional influences. Their emphasis is on correcting nutritional deficiencies and imbalances through diet, lifestyle changes and acupuncture.

Rita is a graduate of the Canadian School of Natural Nutrition (www.csnn.ca) and the Ontario College of Traditional Chinese Medicine (www.OCTCM.com). Upon completion, was granted the designation of RNCP (Registered Nutritional Consulting Practitioner) through the International Organization of Nutritional Consultants (www.ionc.org) and Acupuncturist by the Canadian Society of Chinese Medicine and Acupuncture Association.

Rita's years of experience in the health and fitness industry, coupled with her education and ongoing activities, have inspired her to bring a comprehensive approach to her practice as a Holistic Practitioner. She provides one-on-one consultations, private and corporate consultations, group seminars and wellness workshops.

Most recently, her accomplishments include the publishing of her first cookbook, *Wheat-Free, Dairy-Free Recipes*, and this cookbook. Both are available through Amazon.ca and other online book stores.

Rita can also be found on Rogers TV as a community producer for several shows focusing on digestive health and is a keynote speaker.

Made in the USA
Coppell, TX
21 January 2024

27957821R00062